D[...]

[...]

HAJ
AND
UMRAH

By
Moulana M.S. Banoo (Nadwi)

Islamic Book Service (P) Ltd.

DUAS FOR HAJ AND UMRAH

Author
Moulana M.S. Banoo (Nadwi)

ISBN 978-81-7231-181-0

First Published 2000
Fourteenth Impression 2013
Revised Edition 2014
Second Impression 2016

Published by *Abdus Sami* for :

Islamic Book Service (P) Ltd.

1511-12, Pataudi House, Darya Ganj, New Delhi-2 (India)
Tel.: +91-11-23244556, 23253514, 23269050, 23286551
e-mail: info@ibsbookstore.com
Website: www.ibsbookstore.com
amazon.in www.bit.do/ibs

OUR ASSOCIATES

Al Mashkoor Bookshop LLC, **Sharjah (U.A.E.)**
Azhar Academy Ltd., **London (United Kingdom)**
Lautan Lestari (Lestari Books), **Jakarta (Indonesia)**
Husami Book Depot, **Hyderabad (India)**

Printed in India

DEDICATION

To my parents

Ghulam Hussain Banoo,
Rahmat Bibi Banoo,
and my late Sheikh
Abul Hasan Ali Nadwi

(May Allay grant the Jannah)

CONTENTS

بِسْمِ اللهِ الرَّحْمٰنِ الرَّحِيمِ

نَحْمَدُهُ وَنُصَلِّى عَلٰى رَسُوْلِهِ الْكَرِيْمِ

ACKNOWLEDGEMENT

After having written Kitabul Umrah and
Kitabul Haj, many friends requested that
duas therein were limited. If anybody
wished to read more duas (in Arabic with
English translation) relating to Haj or
Umrah no other book was readily
available. This made me realise that a
book on duas (prayers) for the pilgrim
(Haj or Umrah) was needed. When I went
for Haj in 1986 I came across two
excellent pieces of work relating to duas in
Haj. The first was "Book of Haj and
Umrah" by Allamah Qutbuddin Hanafi.
This work has been attached to certain
editions of Irshadus Sari, a famous book
on Haj and Umrah. The second book was a
commentary on Al Azkar called

"Alfutuhat ar Rabbaniyah" by Allama Muhammad bin Alan Shafi (died 1047 A H). The Al-Azkar is a famous book on duas from the Hadith by the great Muhaddith Mohiyuddin Abu Zakariya An Nuwawi (died 676 AH).

I have also referrd to a few other books but found that they have mostly taken extracts from the work of the two aforementioned scholars. The duas range from leaving home till one's return. **Some of the duas are masnoon (according to the teachings of Rasulullah ﷺ while others are to suit the occasion especially in Haj**.

In Haj only a small amount of duas have been recorded from the Prophet ﷺ. The balance are duas made by the Sahaba رضى الله تعالى عنهم, Tabi'een and the pious. It is obvious that the two learned collators only took duas that were of a hight quality and had some effect in them. Therefore I wish to categorically state that (a) all the duas are not masnoon; (b) the Haji or Mutamir is not bound to read these duas as they appear. If he does not find this collection suitable, he can recite whatever pleases him. (c) Some duas have been taken from the Qur'an and Hadith but are of a general nature.

When selecting the duas I took those duas which fulfil one's basic needs in this world and the Hereafter. The pilgrim can also make dua in his own language. Arabic is the language of the Qur'an and the Hadith. To make dua to Allah in His beloved language deserves merit. Also chosen were duas of a compact nature. The Prophet ﷺ loved duas that were compact serving the needs of the Dunya (this world) and the Akhirah (Hereafter). As an example the Rabbana Atina fid

Dunya was one dua that the Prophet ﷺ read excessively.

The translator is placed in an akward position when it comes to translating prayers (duas) into English. Each language has its own style of expression. The English in this booklet might seem a little bit clumsy and literally incorrect as I did not attempt a free translation. I kept to the actual Arabic text as far as possible. The pilgrim is not expected to memorise all the duas. He can recite it direct from the book. **The labbaik must be memorised.**

INTRODUCTION

The journey to Makkah and Madinah is no ordinary trip. One visits extremely sacred places and passes through moments in which Allah accepts duas (prayers). A list of places and times of acceptance is given hereunder. Therefore one has to strive in dua at all times in these places otherwise the journey will be a fruitless exercise. Apart from sacred places the Haji/ Mutamir also occupies a special position in the eyes of Allah.

Abu Hurairah رضى الله تعالى عنه reports from Rasulullah ﷺ that "The Haji and Mutamir are the guests of Allah. When they make dua unto Him, He accepts, and when they seek His Pardon, He forgives them.   *[Ibn Majah]*

Allah also says in the Qur'an:

"Call unto me and I will reply to You."

[Qur'an 40:60]. This verse is of a general nature applying to all. From the above Hadith we make out that the pilgrim enjoys a special closeness to Allah with a virtual guarantee of acceptance. The pilgrim must not regard this is a blank cheque but certain conditions govern this promise of Allah. These are mentioned further on and also a warning to those whose duas are not accepted. We read in the Qur'an of Shaitan making a request to Allah and that his request is granted by Allah.   *[See Qur'an Ch.7 V.14-15]*

Despite the fact that Shaitan had already fallen from the Grace of Allah.

If Allah could grant that rebel a wish, will He not accept the requests of a member of the Ummah of Muhammad ﷺ who has left his home and dear ones to be present in the barren precincts of Makkah calling out to his Creator "I am present, O' Allah I am present." Therefore dear pilgrim try your best and make as much dua as possible whilst in the Haramain Sharifain (The Two Sacred Places).

A large amount of sayings of the Prophet ﷺ also exhort the believer to turn to his Creator. In fact one Hadith says.

"Dua (prayer) is also a form of worship."
[Abu Daud/Tirmizi]

A few etiquettes of dua are mentioned here:

(i)   Where possible face the Qiblah *

(ii)   Recite the dua in a moderate tone

(iii) Be Humble and imploring to Allah

(iv)   Repeat the dua thrice

(v)   Hope for acceptance but do not expect immediate results.

(vi)   Be attentive while making dua

---

* Whilst making Tawaf one should not face or look at the Ka'bah.

(vii) Begin every dua Praising Allah, sending Blessings to the Holy Prophet ﷺ (Salat alan Nabi/ Durood) and end the prayer with Salat alan Nabi/Durood and Praise of Allah.

Finally, and the most important: before departure.

Repentance, settling any outstanding wrongs or dealings with others and turning towards one's Lord.

Duas are not accepted of those people whose earnings are haram (unlawful). Islam has laid great stress on earning an honest living. Here are some common areas of haram. (This is not an extensive list.)

(1) Living off interest

(2) Gambling

(3) Buying and selling of stolen property

(4) Usurping estates from the lawful heirs

(5) Dealing in alcoholic drinks (Including being employed by a brewery.)

(6) Proceeds from prostitution and pornography.

Dear Muslim brother and sister, beware of haram earnings for it shuts one off from the Creator.

A person going for Haj or Umrah whilst indulging in any of the above will not return a purified man but probably worse in outlook. Allah save us from all evil.

Times when duas are accepted:

a) Friday

b) The last third portion of the night

c) When it rains

d) When salah is about to start and after salah

e) On seeing the Ka'bah.

Places where duas are accepted:

(1) Arafat on the 9th of Zil Haj

(2) Mina (especially after stoning the Ist and second Jamarahs on the 11th/12th and 13th of Zil Haj.)

(3) At the Multazam

(4) The well of Zam Zam (Closed)

(5) Safa-Marwah and in between the two

(6) In the Ka'bah

(7) The Hatim

(8) The Rukn Yamani

(9) The Hajr Aswad

(10) Muzdalifah the last portion of the night and between fajr azaan and sunrise. (10th Zil Haj)

(11) When drinking Zam Zam.

Dear pilgrim: Do not restrict yourself to duas at specific locations. You can read this booklet whilst sitting in the Haram Sharif or anywhere else.

The reader is also advised to use my publications, "Kitabul Haj" or "Kitabul Umrah" as it contains several diagrams of interest and importance to the pilgrim.

The compiler and publishers of this book humbly request the readers to make dua for them in the sacred places and if you go to Madinah convey our salaams at the Most Holy and Purified Grave of the Nabi (ﷺ).

"Our Lord, accept from us (this effort) and forgive us, surely You are the Forgiving and Merciful."

وَالسَّلَامُ

M.S. Banoo (Nadwi)
8th August 2014 – 11th Shawwal 1435

13 Topaas Street, Ext. 5,
Lenasia - 1827, Republic of South Africa
Phone : (011) 854 4664 | Mob.: 27835864831
Email : msbanoo@maktabathome.com
Website : www.maktabathome.com

NOTE

The word Subhan has been translated as Glory (unto Allah) A closer and more correct meaning is "Pure from faults and imperfection" "immaculate" "free of defects."

(1) ON LEAVING HOME

بِسْمِ اللهِ تَوَكَّلْتُ عَلَى اللهِ
وَلَا حَوْلَ وَلَا قُوَّةَ اِلَّا بِاللهِ۔

In the Name of Allah.

I rely upon Allah. There is no power or might except from Allah.

(2) FOR JOURNEY

اَللّٰهُمَّ اِنَّا نَسْئَلُكَ فِيْ سَفَرِنَا هٰذَا اَلْبِرَّ
وَالتَّقْوٰى وَمِنَ الْعَمَلِ مَا تَرْضٰى۔
اَللّٰهُمَّ هَوِّنْ عَلَيْنَا سَفَرَنَا هٰذَا وَاطْوِ عَنَّا
بُعْدَهٗ، اَللّٰهُمَّ اَنْتَ الصَّاحِبُ فِي السَّفَرِ
وَالْخَلِيْفَةُ فِي الْاَهْلِ، اَللّٰهُمَّ اِنِّيْ اَعُوْذُبِكَ مِنْ

وَعَثَآءِ السَّفَرِ وَكَآبَةِ الْمَنْظَرِ وَسُوْءِ

الْمُنْقَلَبِ فِي الْمَالِ وَالْأَهْلِ۔

O Allah, surely we ask of You in this journey of ours, good and piety and of those actions which please You. O Allah, make easy this journey of ours and shorten it's length.

O Allah, You are (our) Companion in journey and Caretaker in the home. O Allah, I seek protection in You from the hardship of travel, evil sights and of an evil return to (our) possessions and family.

(3) WHEN BOARDING A VEHICLE/ PLANE ETC.

اَللّٰهُ اَكْبَرُ اللّٰهُ اَكْبَرُ اللّٰهُ اَكْبَرُ الْحَمْدُ لِلّٰهِ سُبْحَانَ

الَّذِيْ سَخَّرَلَنَا هٰذَا وَمَا كُنَّا لَهٗ مُقْرِنِيْنَ وَاِنَّا

اِلٰى رَبِّنَا لَمُنْقَلِبُوْنَ ۚ

Allah is the Greatest. Allah is the Greatest. Allah is the Greatest. All praise is due to Allah. Glory unto Him who controlled this for us whilst we were unable to control it. Surely our return is to our Lord.

(4) FEAR DURING JOURNEY

اَللّٰهُمَّ اِنَّا نَجْعَلُكَ فِيْ نُحُوْرِهِمْ وَنَعُوْذُبِكَ مِنْ شُرُوْرِهِمْ ۚ

O Allah, we place you in their (enemy) advance and we seek protection in You from their evil.

(5) INTENTION FOR UMRAH

اَللّٰهُمَّ اِنِّيْ اُرِيْدُ الْعُمْرَةَ فَيَسِّرْهَا لِيْ وَتَقَبَّلْهَا مِنِّيْ ۚ

O Allah, I am intending to make Umrah, so make it easy for me and accept the Umrah from me.

(6) INTENTION FOR HAJ AND UMRAH (FOR QIRAN HAJ)

اَللّٰهُمَّ اِنِّیْ اُرِیْدُ الْعُمْرَةَ وَالْحَجَّ فَیَسِّرْهُمَا لِیْ وَتَقَبَّلْهُمَا مِنِّیْ، لَبَّیْكَ بِحَجَّةٍ وَّعُمْرَةٍ۔

O Allah, I intend performing Umrah and Haj, so make both easy for me and accept them from me. I am present for Haj and Umrah.

(7) INTENTION FOR HAJ (TAMATTU/ IFRAD)

اَللّٰهُمَّ اِنِّیْ اُرِیْدُ الْحَجَّ فَیَسِّرْهُ لِیْ وَتَقَبَّلْهُ مِنِّیْ،

O Allah, I intend (performing) Haj, so make it easy for me and accept it from me.

(8) THE TALBIYAH

لَبَّيْكَ اَللّٰهُمَّ لَبَّيْكَ

لَبَّيْكَ لَا شَرِيْكَ لَكَ لَبَّيْكَ

إِنَّ الْحَمْدَ وَالنِّعْمَةَ لَكَ وَالْمُلْكَ

لَا شَرِيْكَ لَكَ.

Here I am, O Allah, here I am.

Here I am. You have no partner, here I am.

Surely all praise, favour and authority belong to You.

You have no partner.

لَبَّيْكَ اِلٰهَ الْخَلْقِ لَبَّيْكَ، لَبَّيْكَ غَفَّارَ

الذُّنُوْبِ لَبَّيْكَ، لَبَّيْكَ وَسَعْدَيْكَ وَالْخَيْرُ

كُلُّهُ بِيَدَيْكَ وَالرَّغْبَآءُ إِلَيْكَ وَالْعَمَلُ لَبَّيْكَ

حَقًّا حَقًّا تَعَبُّدًا وَرِقًّا.

I am present, God of the Creation. I am present.

I am present, Forgiver of Sins.

I am present.

I am present and at Your Service.

All good is in Your Hands.

My keeness and action is for You.

I am present in servitude and bondage (unto You).

(If you wish to read more than the Talbiyah, the second dua could also be read).

(9) DUA AFTER SALATUL IHRAM

اَللّٰهُمَّ اِنِّیْ اَسْئَلُكَ رِضَاكَ وَالْجَنَّةَ وَاَعُوْذُبِكَ مِنْ غَضَبِكَ وَالنَّارِ۔

O Allah! I seek Your Pleasure and Jannah (Paradise) and I Seek Your Protection from Your Anger and the Fire.

(10) DUA OUTSIDE MAKKAH

اَللّٰهُمَّ اِنَّ هٰذَا حَرَمُكَ وَحَرَمُ رَسُوْلِكَ فَحَرِّمْ
لَحْمِيْ وَدَمِيْ وَعَظْمِيْ وَ بَشَرِيْ عَلَى النَّارِ،
اَللّٰهُمَّ اٰمِنِّيْ عَذَابَكَ يَوْمَ تُبْعَثُ عِبَادُكَ.

O Allah! Surely this is Your Sacred Place
and the Sacred Place of Your Prophet. So
forbid the fire upon my flesh, blood, bones
and skin. O Allah! Grant me protection
from Your Punishment on the Day on
which Your servants will be raised.

اَللّٰهُمَّ الْبَلَدُ بَلَدُكَ وَالْبَيْتُ بَيْتُكَ جِئْتُ
اَطْلُبُ رَحْمَتَكَ وَاَلْزَمُ طَاعَتَكَ مُتَّبِعًا
لِّاَمْرِكَ رَاضِيًا بِقُدَرَتِكَ مُسْتَسْلِمًا لِّاَمْرِكَ
اَسْئَلُكَ مَسْئَلَةَ الْمُضْطَرِّ اِلَيْكَ الْمُشْفِقِ مِنْ
عَذَابِكَ خَآئِفًا لِّعُقُوْبَتِكَ اَنْ تَسْتَقْبِلَنِيْ

بِعَفْوِكَ وَاَنْ تَتَجَاوَزَعَنِّى بِرَحْمَتِكَ وَ اَنْ
تُدْخِلَنِى جَنَّتَكَ۔

O Allah, the Town (Makkah) is Your Town
and the House (Ka'bah) is Your House, I
have come seeking Your Mercy holding
on to Your obedience, following Your
Order, pleased with Your Decree,
Submitting to Your Command, I am
asking of You the request of a distressed
one (unto You), trembling of Your
punishment, fearing Your Wrath, (asking)
that You engulf me with Your Pardon, with
Your Mercy, forgive me and that You
place me in Your Paradise.

(11) WHEN ENTERING MASJIDUL HARAAM / OR ANY OTHER MASJID

بِسْمِ اللهِ اَللّٰهُمَّ صَلِّ عَلٰى مُحَمَّدٍ، اَللّٰهُمَّ اغْفِرْ
لِى ذُنُوبِى وَافْتَحْ لِى اَبْوَابَ رَحْمَتِكَ۔

In the name of Allah. O Allah! Shower Your Mercy upon Muhammad ﷺ O Allah! Forgive my sins and open for me the doors of Your Mercy.

DUA FOR I'TIKAF (NAFL)

نَوَيْتُ الْاِعْتِكَافَ مَا دُمْتُ فِى الْمَسْجِدِ ۔

I intend I'tikaf in the masjid as long as I am present (here).

(12) WHEN LEAVING THE MASJIDUL HARAAM OR ANY OTHER MASJID

بِسْمِ اللهِ، اَللّٰهُمَّ صَلِّ عَلٰى مُحَمَّدٍ اَللّٰهُمَّ اِنِّى اَسْئَلُكَ مِنْ فَضْلِكَ ۔

In the name of Allah. O Allah! Shower Your Mercy on Muhammad ﷺ O Allah! I surely seek from You Your bounty.

(13) ON SIGHTING THE KA'BAH

اَللّٰهُمَّ اَنْتَ السَّلَامُ وَ مِنْكَ السَّلَامُ فَحَيِّنَا

رَبَّنَا بِالسَّلَامِ، اَللّٰهُمَّ زِدْ هٰذَا الْبَيْتَ

تَشْرِيْفًا وَّ تَعْظِيْمًا وَّ تَكْرِيْمًا وَّ مَهَابَةً وَّ زِدْ مَنْ

شَرَّفَهُ وَ كَرَّمَهُ مِمَّنْ حَجَّهُ اَوِ اعْتَمَرَهُ تَشْرِيْفًا وَّ

تَعْظِيْمًا وَّ تَكْرِيْمًا وَّ بِرًّا ۔

O Allah! You are Peace and from You comes Peace. So keep us alive, our Lord in peace. O Allah increase This House dignity, honour, nobility and awe. And, increase him who performs Haj or Umrah in dignity, honour, nobility and piety.

(14) INTENTION FOR TAWAF

اَللّٰهُمَّ اِنِّيْ اُرِيْدُ طَوَافَ بَيْتِكَ الْحَرَامِ

فَيَسِّرْهُ لِيْ وَتَقَبَّلْهُ مِنِّيْ سَبْعَةَ اَشْوَاطٍ

لِلّٰهِ تَعَالٰى۔

O Allah! I intend performing the Tawaf of Your Sacred House, so make my Tawaf easy for me and accept it from me. Seven rounds for Allah, the Most High.

(15) WHEN STARTING TAWAF
(anyone or both)

بِسْمِ اللهِ اللهُ اَكْبَرُ

In the name of Allah-Allah is the Greatest.

بِسْمِ اللهِ وَاللهُ اَكْبَرُ اَللّٰهُمَّ اِيْمَانًا بِكَ وَ

تَصْدِيْقًا بِكِتَابِكَ وَوَفَآءً بِعَهْدِكَ وَ اِتِّبَاعًا

لِسُنَّةِ نَبِيِّكَ۔

(I begin) in the name of Allah and Allah is the Greatest. O Allah, having faith in You, confirming Your Book, being faithful to

Your Promise and following the way of Your Prophet ﷺ.

(16) TAWAF DUAS

رَبَّنَآ اٰتِنَا فِى الدُّنْيَا حَسَنَةً وَّفِى الْاٰخِرَةِ حَسَنَةً وَّقِنَا عَذَابَ النَّارِ۔

Our Lord grant us good in this world and the Hereafter. And save us from the punishment of the fire.

سُبْحَانَ اللهِ وَالْحَمْدُ لِلّٰهِ وَلَآ اِلٰهَ اِلَّا اللهُ وَاللهُ اَكْبَرُ وَلَا حَوْلَ وَلَا قُوَّةَ اِلَّا بِاللهِ الْعَلِيِّ الْعَظِيمِ۔

Glory be to Allah. All praise be to Allah. There is none worthy of worship besides Allah. Allah is the Greatest. There is no power and might except from Allah, the Most High, The Great.

اَللّٰهُمَّ اِنِّيْ اَسْئَلُكَ الرَّاحَةَ عِنْدَ الْمَوْتِ وَالْعَفْوَ عِنْدَالْحِسَابِ۔

O Allah, I seek comfort at the time of death and forgiveness at the time of reckoning.

اَللّٰهُمَّ قَنِّعْنِيْ بِمَا رَزَقْتَنِيْ وَبَارِكْ لِيْ فِيْهِ وَاخْلُفْ عَلٰى كُلِّ غَآئِبَةٍ لِّيْ بِخَيْرٍ۔

O Allah! Make me content with that which You have given me and bless me in it and be my deputy in the welfare of all those who are away from me.

اَللّٰهُمَّ اِنِّيْ اَسْئَلُكَ الْعَفْوَ وَالْعَافِيَةَ فِى الدُّنْيَا وَالْاٰخِرَةِ رَبَّنَآ اٰتِنَا فِى الدُّنْيَا حَسَنَةً وَّفِى الْاٰخِرَةِ حَسَنَةً وَّقِنَا عَذَابَ النَّارِ۔

O Allah, I ask You for forgiveness and safety in the world and in the Hereafter. Our Lord, Grant us Good in the world and in the Hereafter and save us from the punishment of the Fire.

اَللّٰهُمَّ اِنِّیْ اَعُوْذُبِكَ مِنَ الْكُفْرِ وَالْفَاقَةِ وَمَوَاقِفِ الْخِزْيِ فِی الدُّنْیَا وَالْاٰخِرَةِ ۔

O Allah, I seek protection in You from disbelief, hunger and disgrace in the world and in the Hereafter.

اَللّٰهُمَّ اجْعَلْهُ حَجًّا مَّبْرُوْرًا وَذَنْبًا مَّغْفُوْرًا وَسَعْیًا مَّشْكُوْرًا وَعَمَلًا مَّقْبُوْلًا وَتِجَارَةً لَّنْ تَبُوْرَ یَا عَزِیْزُ یَا غَفَّارُ یَا عَالِمَ بِمَا فِی الصُّدُوْرِ نَجِّنَا مِنَ الظُّلُمَاتِ اِلَی النُّوْرِ ۔

O Allah, make it an acceptable Haj,
forgiveness of sins, a rewarding effort, an
acceptable and never failing transaction.
O Most Powerful, O Forgiver, O Knower
of that which is in the hearts, guide us from
the darkness unto light.

اَللّٰهُمَّ اِنَّ الْبَيْتَ بَيْتُكَ وَالْحَرَمَ حَرَمُكَ
وَالْاَمْنَ اَمْنُكَ وَهٰذَا مَقَامُ الْعَآئِذِ بِكَ
مِنَ النَّارِ ۔

O Allah, surely (this) House is Your House
and the Sanctuary is Your Sanctuary, and
Peace is Your Peace and this (place) is the
place of the seeker of protection in You
from the Fire.

اَللّٰهُمَّ اِنِّيْ اَعُوْذُبِكَ مِنَ الشَّكِّ وَالشِّرْكِ
وَالشِّقَاقِ وَالنِّفَاقِ وَسُوْءِ الْاَخْلَاقِ وَسُوْءِ
الْمَنْظَرِ فِي الْمَالِ وَالْاَهْلِ وَالْوَلَدِ ۔

O Allah, I seek protection in you from doubt, from associating partners (with you), dissension, hypocrisy, bad manners, and an evil sight (destruction) in (my) possessions, family and offspring.

اَللّٰهُمَّ اَظِلَّنِیْ تَحْتَ ظِلِّ عَرْشِكَ یَوْمَ لَا ظِلَّ اِلَّا ظِلُّكَ وَاَسْقِنِیْ بِكَاْسِ مُحَمَّدٍ شَرْبَةً هَنِیْئًا لَا اَظْمَاءُ بَعْدَهٗ یَاذَاالْجَلَالِ وَالْاِكْرَامِ ۔

O Allah, grant me shade in the shadow of Your Throne on (such) a day when there will be no shade except Yours and grant me a pleasant and filling drink from the cup of Muhammad ﷺ that I may never become thirsty thereafter, O Possessor of Majesty and Nobility.

اَللّٰهُمَّ اِنَّكَ تَعْلَمُ سِرِّیْ وَعَلَانِیَتِیْ فَاقْبَلْ مَعْذِرَتِیْ وَتَعْلَمُ سُؤْلِیْ فَاَعْطِنِیْ حَاجَتِیْ

وَتَعْلَمُ مَا فِيْ نَفْسِيْ فَاغْفِرْلِيْ ذُنُوْبِيْ اَللّٰهُمَّ
اِنِّيْ اَسْئَلُكَ اِيْمَانًا يُّبَاشِرُ قَلْبِيْ وَيَقِيْنًا
صَادِقًا حَتّٰى لَاۤ اَعْلَمَ اَنَّهُ لَا يُصِيْبُنِيْ اِلَّا مَا
كَتَبْتَ لِيْ وَرِضًا بِمَا قَسَمْتَ لِيْ۔

O Allah, Surely You know my inner and my outer self, so accept my plea, You know my request, so grant my need, You know what is in me, so forgive my sins. O Allah, I am asking You of Faith that is attached to the heart and a truthful conviction until I know that nothing will afflict me except that which You have prescribed for me and make me pleased with that which You set out for me.

اَللّٰهُمَّ اَنَا عَبْدُكَ وَابْنُ عَبْدِكَ اَتَيْتُكَ
بِذُنُوْبٍ كَبِيْرَةٍ وَّاَعْمَالٍ سَيِّئَةٍ وَّهٰذَا مَقَامُ

الْعَآئِذِ بِكَ مِنَ النَّارِ فَاغْفِرْلِيْ اِنَّكَ آنْتَ الْغَفُوْرُ الرَّحِيْمُ ۔

O Allah, I am Your slave and the son of Your slave, I have come to You with many major sins and evil acts and this is a place of the seeker of protection in You from the fire, so forgive me. Surely You are the Most Forgiving and Most Merciful.

اَللّٰهُمَّ رَبَّ هٰذَاالْبَيْتِ الْعَتِيْقِ اَعْتِقْ رِقَابَنَا مِنَ النَّارِ وَاَعِذْنَا مِنَ الشَّيْطَانِ الرَّجِيْمِ وَبَارِكْ لَنَا فِيْمَا اَعْطَيْتَنَا اَللّٰهُمَّ اجْعَلْنَا مِنْ اَكْرَمِ وَفْدِكَ عَلَيْكَ ۔

O Allah, Lord of this Ancient House, free our necks from the fire and protect us from Shaitan the Rejected One and bless us in that which You have granted us. O Allah make us among the most honoured visitors that have come unto You.

اَللّٰهُمَّ هٰذَا بَلَدُكَ وَبَيْتُكَ الْحَرَامُ وَالْمَسْجِدُ الْحَرَامُ وَاَنَا عَبْدُكَ وَابْنُ عَبْدِكَ وَابْنُ اَمَتِكَ اٰتَيْتُكَ بِذُنُوبٍ كَثِيْرَةٍ وَخَطَايَا جَمَّةٍ وَاَعْمَالٍ سَيِّئَةٍ وَهٰذَا مَقَامُ الْعَآئِذِبِكَ مِنَ النَّارِ فَاغْفِرْلِيْ اِنَّكَ اَنْتَ الْغَفُوْرُ الرَّحِيْمُ ۔ اَللّٰهُمَّ اِنَّكَ دَعَوْتَ عِبَادَكَ اِلٰى بَيْتِكَ وَقَدْ جِئْتُ طَالِبًا رَحْمَتَكَ وَمُبْتَغِيًا رِضْوَانَكَ وَاَنْتَ مَنَنْتَ عَلَيَّ بِذَالِكَ فَاغْفِرْلِيْ اِنَّكَ عَلٰى كُلِّ شَىْءٍ قَدِيْرٌ ۔

O Allah, this is Your City, Your Sacred House, the Sacred Masjid and I am Your slave, the son of Your slave and the son of Your bondswoman, I have come to You with many sins, evil actions and bad deeds and this is the place of the seeker of protection in You from the fire, so forgive me. Surely You are the Most Forgiving and Most Merciful.

O Allah, You invited Your Servants to Your House and I have come seeking Your Mercy, intending Your Pleasure and You have favoured me with that, so forgive me. Surely You have power over everything.

اَللّٰهُمَّ اِنَّكَ تَرٰى مَكَانِي وَ تَسْمَعُ دُعَآئِي وَ نِدَائِي لَايَخْفٰى عَلَيْكَ شَىْءٌ مِنْ اَمْرِىْ هٰذَا مَقَامُ الْعَائِذِ بِكَ وَاَنَا الْبَائِسُ الْفَقِيْرُ

الْمُسْتَغِيْثُ الْمُقِرُّ بِخَطِيْئَتِهِ الْمُعْتَرِفُ

بِذَنْبِهِ التَّائِبُ اِلٰى رَبِّهٖ فَلَا تَقْطَعْ رَجَائِىْ وَلَا

تُخِبْ اَمَلِىْ يَاۤ اَرْحَمَ الرَّاحِمِيْنَ۔

O Allah, You see my place (condition) and
you hear my prayer and call. None of my
matters can remain hidden from You. This
is the place of the seeker of protection, the
poor, the beggar, the seeker of help,
admitting his weaknesses and accepting
his sins, a repenter unto his Lord, so do not
dash my hopes or destroy my desire, O
Most Merciful of the Merciful.

اَللّٰهُمَّ اَعِذْنِىْ مِنَ الشَّيْطَانِ الرَّجِيْمِ

وَاَعِذْنِىْ مِنْ كُلِّ سُوْءٍ وَّقَنِّعْنِىْ بِمَا رَزَقْتَنِىْ

وَبَارِكْ لِىْ فِيْهِ اَللّٰهُمَّ اجْعَلْنِىْ مِنْ اَكْرَمِ

وَفِدِكَ عَلَيْكَ وَالْزِمْنِي سَبِيلَ الْإِسْتِقَامَةِ
حَتَّى أَلْقَاكَ يَارَبَّ الْعَالَمِينَ.

O Allah, protect me from Shaitan the Rejected One and save me from all evil and grant me satisfaction with that which you have sustained me with and bless me in it. O Allah make me among the noblest of Your guests and hold me firmly on the straight path until I meet You O Lord of the Universe.

اَللّٰهُمَّ أَعْصِمْنَا بِدِينِكَ وَطَوَاعِيَتِكَ
وَطَوَاعِيَةِ رَسُولِكَ وَجَنِّبْنَا حُدُودَكَ
اَللّٰهُمَّ اجْعَلْنَا نُحِبُّكَ وَنُحِبُّ مَلَآئِكَتَكَ
وَأَنْبِيَآءَكَ وَرُسُلَكَ وَنُحِبُّ عِبَادَكَ
الصَّالِحِينَ.

اَللّٰهُمَّ يَسِّرْنَا الْيُسْرٰى وَجَنِّبْنَا الْعُسْرٰى وَاغْفِرْلَنَا فِى الْاٰخِرَةِ وَالْاُوْلٰى وَاجْعَلْنَا مِنْ اَئِمَّةِ الْمُتَّقِيْنَ۔

O Allah, save us through Your Religion, and obedience to You and the Prophet ﷺ and save us from Your Limits (the forbidden). O Allah, make us love You, Your angels, Your Prophets, Your Messengers and love Your pious slaves.

O Allah, simplify even more the easy, save us from the difficult, forgive us in the Hereafter and the First (the world) and make us leaders of the pious.

يَا مُقَلِّبَ الْقُلُوْبِ ثَبِّتْ قَلْبِى عَلٰى دِيْنِكَ اَللّٰهُمَّ اِنِّىْ اَسْئَلُكَ مُوْجِبَاتِ رَحْمَتِكَ

وَعَزَآئِمَ مَغْفِرَتِكَ وَالسَّلَامَةَ مِنْ كُلِّ إِثْمٍ وَالْفَوْزَ بِالْجَنَّةِ وَالنَّجَاةَ مِنَ النَّارِ اَللّٰهُمَّ اِنِّىْ اَسْئَلُكَ الْهُدٰى وَالتُّقٰى وَالْعِفٰى اَللّٰهُمَّ اَعِنِّىْ عَلٰى ذِكْرِكَ وَشُكْرِكَ وَحُسْنِ عِبَادَتِكَ اَللّٰهُمَّ اِنِّىْ اَسْئَلُكَ مِنَ الْخَيْرِ كُلِّهٖ مَا عَلِمْتُ مِنْهُ وَمَا لَمْ اَعْلَمْ وَ اَسْئَلُكَ الْجَنَّةَ وَمَا قَرَّبَ اِلَيْهَا مِنْ قَوْلٍ اَوْ عَمَلٍ وَاَعُوْذُبِكَ مِنَ النَّارِ وَمَا قَرَّبَ اِلَيْهَا مِنْ قَوْلٍ اَوْ عَمَلٍ۔

O Turner of hearts, make my heart firm upon Your religion. O Allah, I am asking You (that) which confirms Your Mercy, Your steadfast forgiveness. safety from every sin, success with Paradise and salvation from the Fire.

O Allah, I ask for guidance, Piety and wealth.

O Allah, assist me with Your Remembrance, Thankfulness and worshipping You well.

O Allah, I ask You all that is good which I have and do not have knowledge of and I am asking of You Paradise and that which brings one closer to it by means of speech and action.

I seek protection in You from the Fire and that which brings one closer to it by means of speech and action.

يَارَبَّ الْبَيْتِ الْعَتِيقِ اَعْتِقْ رِقَابَنَا وَ
رِقَابَ اٰبَآءِنَاوَ اُمَّهَاتِنَا مِنَ النَّارِ ۔

O Lord of the Ancient House (Ka'bah), free our necks and the necks of our fathers and mothers from the fire.

اَللّٰهُمَّ اِنَّا نَسْئَلُكَ مِنْ كُلِّ خَيْرٍ مَا سَاَلَكَ

مِنْهُ نَبِيُّكَ مُحَمَّدٌ صَلَّى اللهُ عَلَيْهِ وَسَلَّمَ ۔ وَ
نَعُوْذُبِكَ مِنْ كُلِّ شَرٍّ مَا اسْتَعَاذَكَ مِنْهُ
نَبِيُّكَ مُحَمَّدٌ صَلَّى اللهُ عَلَيْهِ وَسَلَّمَ ۔

O Allah, we seek from You all the good which Your Nabi Muhammad ﷺ sought from You and we seek Your Protection from all the evil that Your Nabi Muhammad ﷺ sought protection from in You.

رَبَّنَا لَا تُؤَاخِذْنَا إِنْ نَّسِيْنَا أَوْ أَخْطَأْنَا ۚ رَبَّنَا
وَلَا تَحْمِلْ عَلَيْنَا إِصْرًا كَمَا حَمَلْتَهُ عَلَى
الَّذِيْنَ مِنْ قَبْلِنَا ۚ رَبَّنَا وَلَا تُحَمِّلْنَا مَا لَا
طَاقَةَ لَنَا بِهٖ ۚ وَاعْفُ عَنَّا ۖ وَاغْفِرْ لَنَا ۖ
وَارْحَمْنَا ۚ أَنْتَ مَوْلٰنَا فَانْصُرْنَا عَلَى الْقَوْمِ
الْكٰفِرِيْنَ ۞

Our Lord! Punish us not if we forget or miss our mark. Our Lord, do not burden us as You have placed burdens on those before us.

Our Lord! Impose not on us that which we do not have the strength to bear. Pardon us, forgive us and have mercy on us. You are our Protector so grant us victory over the disbelievers.

رَبَّنَآ اَفْرِغْ عَلَيْنَا صَبْرًا وَّ تَوَفَّنَا مُسْلِمِيْنَ.

Our Lord! Bestow on us patience and make us die Muslims.

اَللّٰهُمَّ اِنَّا نَسْئَلُكَ اِيْمَانًا خَالِصًا وَّ قَلْبًا خَاشِعًا وَّ نَسْئَلُكَ عِلْمًا نَافِعًا وَّ يَقِيْنًا صَادِقًا وَّ دِيْنًا قَيِّمًا وَّ نَسْئَلُكَ الْعَفْوَ وَالْعَافِيَةَ وَ نَسْئَلُكَ دَوَامَ الْعَافِيَةِ وَ

نَسْئَلُكَ الشُّكْرَ عَلَى الْعَافِيَةِ وَ نَسْئَلُكَ
الْغِنٰى عَنِ النَّاسِ ۔

O Allah, we ask of You a pure faith, a
humble heart, beneficial knowledge, true
conviction, steadfastness, forgiveness and
safety from all tests, a continuous safety
and we also ask of You thankfulness for
safety (granted to us) and independence
from people.

اَللّٰهُمَّ اَحْيِنِيْ عَلٰى سُنَّةِ رَسُوْلِكَ مُحَمَّدٍ صَلَّى
اللهُ عَلَيْهِ وَسَلَّمَ وَتَوَفَّنِيْ مُسْلِمًا وَّالْحِقْنِيْ
بِالصَّالِحِيْنَ وَاجْعَلْنِيْ مِنْ وَّرَثَةِ جَنَّةِ النَّعِيْمِ
وَاغْفِرْلِيْ خَطِيْئَتِيْ يَوْمَ الدِّيْنِ ۔

O Allah, keep me alive (that I follow) the
way of Your Nabi Muhammad ﷺ and

make me die a muslim, join me to the
pious and make me of the inheritors of
paradise and forgive my sins on the Day of
Reckoning.

(17) AT MAQAM IBRAHIM

وَاتَّخِذُوْا مِنْ مَّقَامِ اِبْرَاهِيْمَ مُصَلًّى ۔

Take as your place of worship the place
where Ibrahim (عَلَيْهِ الصَّلَاةُ وَالسَّلَام) stood (to perform
Salah).   *[Surah Baqarah: 125]*

(18) WHEN DRINKING ZAM ZAM

اَللّٰهُمَّ اِنِّیْۤ اَسْئَلُكَ عِلْمًا نَّافِعًا وَّرِزْقًا وَّاسِعًا

وَّشِفَآءً مِّنْ كُلِّ دَآءٍ ۔

O Allah, I am asking You for beneficial
knowledge an extensive sustenance and
cure from all ills.

At the Multazam pour out the essence of your requests in this world and the Hereafter.

Remember us also in your duas.

(19) AT SAFA

اَبَدَأُ بِمَا بَدَأَ اللهُ بِهِ اِنَّ الصَّفَا وَالْمَرْوَةَ مِنْ شَعَآئِرِ اللهِ۔

لَاۤ اِلٰهَ اِلَّا اللهُ۔

اَللهُ اَكْبَرُ اللهُ اَكْبَرُ اللهُ اَكْبَرُ وَ لِلّٰهِ الْحَمْدُ اَلْحَمْدُ لِلّٰهِ عَلَى مَا هَدَانَا، اَلْحَمْدُ لِلّٰهِ عَلَى مَا اَوْلَانَا، اَلْحَمْدُ لِلّٰهِ عَلَى مَا اَلْهَمَنَا۔

اَلْحَمْدُ لِلّٰهِ الَّذِىْ هَدَانَا لِهٰذَا وَمَا كُنَّا

لِنَهْتَدِيَ لَوْلَا أَنْ هَدَانَا اللهُ۔

لَا إِلٰهَ إِلَّا اللهُ وَحْدَهُ لَا شَرِيكَ لَهُ لَهُ الْمُلْكُ

وَلَهُ الْحَمْدُ، يُحْيِى وَيُمِيتُ وَهُوَ عَلَى كُلِّ شَيْءٍ

قَدِيرٌ لَا إِلٰهَ إِلَّا اللهُ وَحْدَهُ وَنَصَرَ عَبْدَهُ وَهَزَمَ

الْأَحْزَابَ وَحْدَهُ۔

لَا إِلٰهَ إِلَّا اللهُ وَلَا نَعْبُدُ إِلَّا إِيَّاهُ مُخْلِصِينَ لَهُ

الدِّينَ وَلَوْ كَرِهَ الْكَافِرُونَ اللّٰهُمَّ كَمَا

هَدَيْتَنِى لِلْإِسْلَامِ أَسْئَلُكَ أَنْ لَّا تَنْزِعَهُ

مِنِّى حَتَّى تَوَفَّانِى وَأَنَا مُسْلِمٌ سُبْحَانَ اللهِ

وَالْحَمْدُ للهِ وَلَا إِلٰهَ إِلَّا اللهُ اللهُ أَكْبَرُ وَلَا حَوْلَ

وَلَا قُوَّةَ إِلَّا بِاللهِ الْعَلِيِّ الْعَظِيمِ۔

اَللّٰهُمَّ صَلِّ وَ سَلِّمْ عَلٰى سَيِّدِنَا مُحَمَّدٍ وَعَلٰى اٰلِهٖ وَصَحْبِهٖ وَاَتْبَاعِهٖ اِلٰى يَوْمِ الدِّيْنِ وَسَلَامٌ عَلَى الْمُرْسَلِيْنَ وَالْحَمْدُ لِلّٰهِ رَبِّ الْعَالَمِيْنَ ۔

I begin with that which Allah began with "Surely Safa and Marwah are among the Symbols of Allah"

There is no diety (worthy of worship besides Allah.)

Allah is the Greatest.

Allah is the Greatest.

Allah is the Greatest.

All praise is due to Allah upon that which He guided us.

All praise is due to Allah who has bestowed upon us.

All praise is due to Allah who has inspired us.

All praise is due to Allah who has guided us to this (Islam) and we could not reach it if Allah did not guide us.

There is no god (worthy of worship) besides Allah, who is Alone and has no partner.

For Him is All Sovereignty and for Him is All Praise.

He gives life and death and has power over everything.

There is no god (worthy of worship) besides Allah, who is Alone, He has assisted his slave (Muhammad ﷺ) and defeated all groups Alone.

There is no god (worthy of worship) besides Allah and we do not worship but him, sincere in faith to Him even if the disbelivers detest it.

O Allah, as You have guided me to Islam, I ask of you not to take it (Islam) away from me until I die a Muslim.

Glory unto Allah, All praise unto Allah, there is no god (worthy of worship) besides Allah, Allah is the Greatest and there is no power and might except from Allah, The Most High and the Most Mighty.

O Allah, shower Your choicest Blessings and Salutations upon our Leader, Muhammad ﷺ and upon His Family, Companions and Followers till the Day of Judgement.

Peace be upon all the Prophets and all Praise is due to Allah, Lord of the Universe.

(20) BETWEEN SAFA-MARWAH AND AT MARWAH

اَللّٰهُمَّ اغْفِرْ وَارْحَمْ وَاعْفُ عَمَّا تَعْلَمُ وَ اَنْتَ الْاَعَزُّ الْاَكْرَمُ ۔

O Allah, pardon (us), have mercy, forgive that which you Know (about us) and You are the Most Powerful and Most Noble.

اَللّٰهُمَّ اِنِّىْ اَسْئَلُكَ مِنَ الْخَيْرِ كُلِّهٖ عَاجِلِهٖ وَآجِلِهٖ مَا عَلِمْتُ مِنْهُ وَمَا لَمْ اَعْلَمْ ۔

O Allah, I am asking of You all good (be it) immediate or late, that which I am aware of and that which I am unaware of.

اَللّٰهُمَّ لَكَ الْحَمْدُ كُلُّهُ وَلَكَ الْكَمَالُ كُلُّهُ وَلَكَ الْجَلَالُ كُلُّهُ وَلَكَ التَّقْدِيْسُ كُلُّهُ

اَللّٰهُمَّ اغْفِرْلِیْ جَمِیْعَ مَا اَسْلَفْتُهٗ وَاَعْصِمْنِیْ
فِیْمَا بَقِیَ وَارْزُقْنِیْ عَمَلًا صَالِحًا تَرْضٰی بِهٖ عَنِّیْ
یَاذَاالْفَضْلِ الْعَظِیْمِ ۔

O Allah, all praise and all greatness belongs to You, All Majesty and Sanctity is for You.

O Allah, forgive me for all that I have done in the past and save me from that which remains and grant me the opportunity of good deeds which You will be pleased with, O Possessor of Goodness and Might.

اَللّٰهُمَّ بِنُوْرِكَ اِهْتَدَیْنَا وَبِفَضْلِكَ
اِسْتَقْمْنَا وَفِیْ کَنَفِكَ اَصْبَحْنَا وَاَمْسَیْنَا
اَنْتَ الْاَوَّلُ فَلَا شَیْءَ بَعْدَكَ نَعُوْذُبِكَ مِنْ

الْفَلَسِ وَالْكَسَلِ وَمِنْ عَذَابِ الْقَبْرِ وَمِنْ
فِتْنَةِ الْغِنٰى وَالْفَقْرِ ۔

O Allah, with Your Light we found
guidance and with Your Grace we
remained firm and in Your Protection we
begin morning and evening. You are the
First and there is nothing after You. We
seek protection in You from poverty,
laziness, from the punishment of the grave
and the trials of wealth and poverty.

اَللّٰهُمَّ اهْدِنَا اِلَى الْحَقِّ وَاجْعَلْنَا مِنْ اَهْلِهٖ
وَانْصُرْنَا بِهٖ

O Allah, guide us to the truth and make us
from amongst it's (the truth) people and
assist us with it.

اَللّٰهُمَّ اغْسِلْ خَطَايَاىَ بِالْمَآءِ وَالثَّلْجِ وَالْبَرَدِ وَ نَقِّ قَلْبِىْ مِنَ الْخَطَايَا كَمَا يُنَقَّى الثَّوْبُ الْاَبْيَضُ مِنَ الدَّنَسِ وَبَاعِدْ بَيْنِىْ وَ بَيْنَ خَطَايَاىَ كَمَا بَاعَدْتَّ بَيْنَ الْمَشْرِقِ وَالْمَغْرِبِ

O Allah, cleanse my sins with water and ice, cleanse my heart of wrong like dirt which is washed off white clothing and separate me from my sins like You have separated East and West.

اَللّٰهُمَّ اِنِّىْ اَسْئَلُكَ فَوَاتِحَ الْخَيْرِ وَ خَوَاتِمَهٗ وَ جَوَامِعَهٗ وَاَوَّلَهٗ وَاٰخِرَهٗ وَ ظَاهِرَهٗ وَ بَاطِنَهٗ وَالدَّرَجَاتِ الْعُلٰى مِنَ الْجَنَّةِ

O Allah, I ask of You the sources of goodness, It's ending, all of it, the first and last of it and it's outward and inward and the high ranks of Paradise.

رَبِّ اغْفِرْ وَارْحَمْ اَنْتَ الْاَعَزُّ الْاَكْرَمُ ۔

O my Lord! Forgive (us) and be merciful (to us). Surely You are Most Mighty and Most Generous.

اَللّٰهُمَّ صَلِّ عَلٰى مُحَمَّدٍ وَّ عَلٰى اٰلِ مُحَمَّدٍ
وَّبَارِكْ وَسَلِّمْ ۔

O Allah! Shower Your Blessings, Mercies and Salutations on Muhammad ﷺ and the family (followers) of Muhammad ﷺ.

(21) WHEN CUTTING OR SHAVING THE HEAD (UMRAH)

اَلْحَمْدُ لِلّٰهِ عَلٰى مَاهَدَانَا، اَلْحَمْدُ لِلّٰهِ عَلٰى مَا

أَنْعَمَ بِهِ عَلَيْنَا، اَللّٰهُمَّ هٰذِهِ نَاصِيَتِي فَتَقَبَّلْ مِنِّي وَاغْفِرْلِي ذُنُوْبِي اَللّٰهُمَّ اغْفِرْلِي وَلِلْمُحَلِّقِيْنَ وَالْمُقَصِّرِيْنَ يَا وَاسِعَ الْمَغْفِرَةِ. اٰمِيْن

All praise is due to Allah upon that which He guided us. All praise is due to Allah of that which He favoured us with.

O Allah, this is my forehead so accept it from me and forgive my sins.

O Allah, forgive me and those who shave their heads or cut their hair. O Reservoir of Mercy.

(22) TO MINA

اَللّٰهُمَّ اِيَّاكَ اَرْجُوْ وَلَكَ اَدْعُوْ فَبَلِّغْنِي صَالِحَ

اَمَلِّيْ وَاغْفِرْلِيْ ذُنُوْبِيْ وَامْنُنْ عَلَيَّ بِمَا مَنَنْتَ

بِهٖ عَلٰى اَهْلِ طَاعَتِكَ اِنَّكَ عَلٰى كُلِّ شَئٍ قَدِيْرٌ

O Allah, it is You I hope for and You I pray to, so make me fulfil my good goals, forgive me my sins, favour me as You have favoured Your obedient Ones.

Surely You have power over everything.

اَللهُ اَكْبَرُ اَللهُ اَكْبَرُ لَا اِلٰهَ اِلَّا اللهُ وَاللهُ اَكْبَرُ

اَللهُ اَكْبَرُ وَلِلّٰهِ الْحَمْدُ۔

Allah is the Greatest, Allah is the Greatest.

There is no god (worthy of worship) besides Allah and Allah is the Greatest.

Allah is the Greatest and for Him is All Praise.

(The Takbir is recited after every salah

from the 9th morning till the Asr of the 13th of Zil Haj)

(23) TO ARAFAT

اَللّٰهُمَّ اِلَيْكَ تَوَجَّهْتُ وَ عَلَيْكَ تَوَكَّلْتُ وَلِوَجْهِكَ الْكَرِيْمِ اَرَدْتُ فَاجْعَلْ ذَنْبِى مَغْفُوْرًا وَّحَجِّى مَبْرُوْرًا وَّارْحَمْنِى وَلَا تُخَيِّبْنِى وَبَارِكْ لِّى فِى سَفَرِى وَاقْضِ بِعَرَفَاتٍ حَاجَتِى اِنَّكَ عَلٰى كُلِّ شَىْءٍ قَدِيْرٌ۔

O Allah, to You I turn, upon You I rely, and Your Noble Face I intend, so make my sins forgiven, my Haj an accepted one, have mercy upon me, do not make me unsuccessful, bless me in my journey and fulfill my desires at Arafat.

Surely You have power over all things.

(24) AT ARAFAT

لَا إِلٰهَ إِلَّا اللهُ وَحْدَهُ لَا شَرِيْكَ لَهُ لَهُ الْمُلْكُ
وَلَهُ الْحَمْدُ وَهُوَ عَلٰى كُلِّ شَيْءٍ قَدِيْرٌ ۔

There is no god (worthy of worship) besides Allah, who is Alone and has no partner.

Unto Him (belongs) all Sovereignty, for Him is all praise and He has power over everything.

لَا إِلٰهَ إِلَّا اللهُ وَحْدَهُ لَا شَرِيْكَ لَهُ لَهُ الْمُلْكُ وَلَهُ
الْحَمْدُ يُحْيِى وَيُمِيْتُ وَهُوَ عَلٰى كُلِّ شَيْءٍ قَدِيْرٌ

There is no god (worthy of worship) besides Allah, who is Alone and has no partner.

Unto Him (belongs) all Sovereignty, and all Praise is due to Him. He gives life, causes death and has power over everything.

(Above two are the best duas to read at Arafat).

رَبَّنَآ اٰتِنَا فِى الدُّنْيَا حَسَنَةً وَّفِى الْاٰخِرَةِ حَسَنَةً وَّقِنَا عَذَابَ النَّارِ۔

Our Lord, grant us good in this world and the hereafter. And save us from the punishment of the fire.

اَللّٰهُمَّ لَكَ الْحَمْدُ كَالَّذِىْ تَقُوْلُ اللّٰهُمَّ لَكَ صَلَاتِىْ وَنُسُكِىْ وَمَحْيَاىَ وَمَمَاتِىْ وَاِلَيْكَ مَاٰبِىْ وَلَكَ رَبِّىْ تُرَاثِىْ۔

اَللّٰهُمَّ اِنِّىْ اَعُوْذُبِكَ مِنْ عَذَابِ الْقَبْرِ

وَوَسْوَسَةِ الصَّدْرِ وَشَتَاتِ الْأَمْرِ ۔

اَللّٰهُمَّ اِنِّیْ اَعُوْذُبِكَ مِنْ شَرِّ مَا تَجِیْءُ بِهِ الرِّیْحُ ۔

O Allah, All Praise belongs to You as You
say; O Allah for You is my salah, my
sacrifice, my living and my dying. Unto
You is my return and to you my wealth
belongs O my Lord.

O Allah, I seek protection in You from the
punishment of the grave, from doubts of
the chest and from matters going astray
(awry).

O Allah, I seek protection in You from the
evil which the wind brings.

اَللّٰهُمَّ اِنِّیْ ظَلَمْتُ نَفْسِیْ ظُلْمًا كَثِیْرًا وَّ اِنَّهٗ

لَا یَغْفِرُ الذُّنُوْبَ اِلَّا اَنْتَ فَاغْفِرْلِیْ مَغْفِرَةً

مِّنْ عِنْدِكَ وَارْحَمْنِي اِنَّكَ اَنْتَ الْغَفُوْرُ
الرَّحِيْمُ۔

O Allah, I have wronged my soul excessively, surely none can forgive sins except You, so grant me a forgiveness from You and have mercy on me. Surely You are the Most Merciful and the Most Forgiving.

اَللّٰهُمَّ اغْفِرْلِيْ مَغْفِرَةً تُصْلِحُ بِهَا شَأْنِيْ فِي
الدَّارَيْنِ وَارْحَمْنِيْ رَحْمَةً اَسْعَدُ بِهَا فِي
الدَّارَيْنِ وَ تُبْ عَلَيَّ تَوْبَةً نَّصُوْحًا لَا اَنْكُثُهَا
اَبَدًا وَّالْزِمْنِيْ سَبِيْلَ الْاِسْتِقَامَةِ لَا اَزِيْغُ
عَنْهَا اَبَدًا اَللّٰهُمَّ انْقُلْنِيْ مِنْ ذِلِّ الْمَعْصِيَةِ
اِلٰى عِزِّ الطَّاعَةِ وَاَغْنِنِيْ بِحَلَالِكَ عَنْ حَرَامِكَ

وَبِطَاعَتِكَ عَنْ مَعْصِيَتِكَ وَبِفَضْلِكَ عَمَّنْ
سِوَاكَ وَ نَوِّرْ قَلْبِى وَقَبْرِى وَ اَعِذْنِى مِنَ الشَّرِّ
كُلِّهٖ وَ اجْمَعْ لِى الْخَيْرَ كُلَّهٗ ۔

O Allah, grant me such forgiveness that will make good my matter in both worlds, bestow upon me a kindness that will make me blessed in both places, accept a noble repentance from me that I will never ever break, hold me firm on the path of constancy which I will never deviate from.

O Allah, remove me from the depths of disobedience to the lofty heights of obedience and enrich me with pure (earnings) instead of the unlawful, and endow me with obedience in place of rebellion unto You and with Your Grace instead of other, and illuminate my heart and grave and protect me from all evil and gather for me all good.

اَللّٰهُمَّ لَكَ الْحَمْدُ كُلُّهٗ وَلَكَ الشُّكْرُ كُلُّهٗ وَلَكَ الْمُلْكُ كُلُّهٗ اَسْئَلُكَ الْخَيْرَ كُلَّهٗ وَاَعُوْذُبِكَ مِنَ الشَّرِّ كُلِّهٖ ۔

O Allah, unto You belongs all Praise, Gratefulness and Sovereignty. I am asking of you all good and I seek protection in You from all evil.

اَللّٰهُمَّ اغْفِرْلِيْ جَمِيْعَ مَا مَضٰى مِنْ ذُنُوْبِيْ وَاعْصِمْنِيْ فِيْمَا بَقِيَ مِنْ عُمُرِيْ وَارْزُقْنِيْ عَمَلًا زَاكِيًا تَرْضٰى بِهٖ عَنِّيْ ۔

O Allah, forgive all my sins of the past, save me for the rest of my life and grant me the opportunity of pure deeds which will make You pleased with me.

اَللّٰهُمَّ يَسِّرْ لِيَ الْاٰخِرَةَ وَالْاُوْلٰى وَاعْصِمْنِيْ بِاَلْطَافِكَ وَاجْعَلْنِيْ مِمَّنْ يُّحِبُّكَ وَيُحِبُّ رَسُوْلَكَ وَمَلَآئِكَتَكَ وَيُحِبُّ عِبَادَكَ الصَّالِحِيْنَ وَاَوْلِيَآئَكَ الْمُتَّقِيْنَ.

O Allah, make the Hereafter and (this) world easy for me, and protect me with your kindness and make me among those who love You and those who love Your Prophet, the Angels, Your Pious Servants and Your Mindful Friends.

اَللّٰهُمَّ اَحْيِنِيْ عَلٰى سُنَّةِ نَبِيِّكَ مُحَمَّدٍ صَلَّى اللهُ عَلَيْهِ وَسَلَّمَ وَتَوَفَّنِيْ عَلٰى مِلَّتِهٖ وَاَعِذْنِيْ مِنْ مُضِلَّاتِ الْفِتَنِ.

O Allah, keep me alive upon the way of Your Prophet Muhammad ﷺ and make me die within his group and protect me from misleading trials.

اَللّٰهُمَّ اِنِّیْ اَسْتَغْفِرُكَ لِكُلِّ ذَنْبٍ يُّمِيْتُ الْقَلْبَ وَيَشْعَلُ الْكَرَبَ وَ يَشْعَلُ الْفِكْرَ وَ يُرْضَى الشَّيْطَانَ وَيَسْخَطُ الرَّبَّ ۔

O Allah, I am seeking your Pardon from every wrong that destroys the heart, ignites difficulty, increases anxiety, makes Shaitan happy and angers the Lord.

اَللّٰهُمَّ اِنَّكَ اَمَرْتَ بِالدُّعَآءِ وَقَضَيْتَ عَلٰى نَفْسِكَ بِالْاِجَابَةِ وَ اَنْتَ لَا تُخْلِفُ الْمِيْعَادَ وَلَا تَنْكُثُ عَهْدَكَ ۔

O Allah, surely You ordered (us) to prayer
and You decreed upon Yourself to answer.
You do not go against (Your) promise and
You do not break Your Vow.

اَللّٰهُمَّ اِنَّ لِكُلِّ وَفْدٍ جَآئِزَةً وَّ لِكُلِّ زَآئِرٍ

كَرَامَةً وَّلِكُلِّ سَآئِلٍ لَّكَ عَطِيَّةً وَّلِكُلِّ رَاجٍ

لَّكَ ثَوَابًا وَّلِكُلِّ مَنْ فَزِعَ اِلَيْكَ رَحْمَةً وَّلِكُلِّ

مَنْ رَغِبَ فِيْكَ زُلْفٰى وَلِكُلِّ مُتَضَرِّعٍ اِلَيْكَ

اِجَابَةً وَلِكُلِّ مِسْكِيْنٍ اِلَيْكَ رَافَةً وَقَدْ

وَفَدْتُ اِلَيْكَ وَوَقَفْتُ بَيْنَ يَدَيْكَ فِىْ هٰذِهِ

الْمَوَاضِعِ الَّتِىْ شَرَّفْتَهَا رَجَآءً لِّمَا عِنْدَكَ فَلَا

تَجْعَلْنِى الْيَوْمَ اَخْيَبَ وَفْدِكَ وَاَكْرِمْنِىْ

بِالْجَنَّةِ وَمُنَّ عَلَىَّ بِالْمَغْفِرَةِ وَالْعَافِيَةِ وَاَجِرْنِىْ

مِنَ النَّارِ وَوَسِّعْ عَلَىَّ مِنَ الرِّزْقِ الْحَلَالِ
الطَّيِّبِ وَادْرَأْ عَنِّى شَرَّ فِتْنَةِ الْعَرَبِ
وَالْعَجَمِ وَشَرَّ فِتْنَةِ الْإِنْسِ وَالْجِنِّ.

O Allah, for every guest (that comes to You) is a reward, for every visitor an honour, for every beggar a gift, for every hopeful a reward, for all who turn to You in fear a mercy, to every one who gladly comes to You a closeness, for everyone who humbles himself to You an acceptance (of prayer), for every deprived one coming to You a kindness.

O Allah, I have come to You and I have stood in front of You in these places which You have sanctified hoping (to get) that which You have. So make me not the most unfortunate of Your guests, honour me with forgiveness and safety, save me from the fire, bless me with pure, halal (lawful) sustenance and hold off the evil tests of the Arabs and non Arabs and the evil tests of man and Jinn.

اَللّٰهُمَّ انْقُلْنِیْ مِنْ ذِلِّ الْمَعْصِیَةِ اِلٰی عِزِّ الطَّاعَةِ وَاَغْنِنِیْ بِحَلَالِكَ عَنْ حَرَامِكَ وَ بِفَضْلِكَ عَمَّنْ سِوَاكَ وَنَوِّرْ قَلْبِیْ وَ قَبْرِیْ وَاَعِذْنِیْ مِنَ الشَّرِّ كُلِّهِ وَاجْمَعْ لِیَ الْخَیْرَ كُلَّهٗ ۔

O Allah, remove me from the depths of disobedience to heights of obedience and sustain me with Your halal (lawful) not from your haram (unlawful), with Your grace not from others, fill my heart and grave with light, protect me from all evil and gather for me all good.

اَللّٰهُمَّ یَا عَظِیْمُ یَا عَظِیْمُ یَا عَظِیْمُ اِغْفِرْلِیْ

ذَنْبِى الْعَظِيمَ فَاِنَّهُ لَا يَغْفِرُ الذَّنْبَ الْعَظِيمَ اِلَّا الْعَظِيمُ ۔

O Allah, O Great One, O Great One, O Great One, forgive me my great sin, surely a great sin cannot be forgiven except by the Great One.

اَللّٰهُمَّ اِنْ كُنْتَ لَا تَرْحَمُ اِلَّا اَهْلَ طَاعَتِكَ فَاِلٰى مَنْ يَّفْزَعُ الْمُذْنِبُوْنَ ۔

O Allah, if You do not show mercy except to Your obedient ones then where to must the sinners turn to?

اَللّٰهُمَّ اغْفِرْلِىْ جَمِيعَ ذُنُوْبِىْ وَاَصْرِفْنِىْ عَنْ مَوْقِفِىْ هٰذَا مَقْضِىَّ الْحَوَآئِجِ وَهَبْ لِىْ مَا سَاَلْتُ وَحَقِّقْ رَجَآئِىْ فِيْمَا تَمَنَّيْتُ ۔

O Allah, forgive me all my sins and send
me back from here (in such a condition)
with requests granted and confer on me
that which I have asked for and confirm
my desire in that which I am hoping for.

اَللّٰهُمَّ اِنَّكَ هَدَيْتَنِيْ اِلَى الْاِسْلَامِ فَلَا
تَنْزِعُهُ مِنِّيْ حَتّٰى تَقْبَضَنِيْ اِلَيْكَ وَ اَنَا عَلَيْهِ وَ
اَصْرِفْنِيْ عَنْ مَوْقِفِيْ هٰذَا مَقْضِيَّ الْحَوَآئِجِ ۗ

O Allah, You have guided me to Islam, so
do not take it away from me until You have
taken me to You as a muslim and turn me
from this standing place of mine with
requests granted.

اَللّٰهُمَّ لَا تَرُدِّ الْجَمِيْعَ لِاَجْلِيْ وَلَا لِشُؤْمِ ذُنُوْبِيْ
بَلِ ارْحَمْنِيْ وَ تَجَاوَزْ عَنِّيْ بِبَرَكَةِ مَنْ حَضَرَ هُنَا
مِنْ اَوْلِيَآئِكَ وَاَحْبَابِكَ ۔

O Allah, do not reject the multitude for my sake nor for the evil of my sins but have mercy upon me and overlook (my sins), due to blessings of those who have gathered here, amongst Your friends and beloved ones.

اَللّٰهُمَّ لَا تَجْعَلْ هٰذَا اٰخِرَ عَهْدِيْ مِنْ هٰذَا الْمَوْقِفِ الْعَظِيْمِ وَارْزُقْنَا الرُّجُوْعَ اِلَيْهِ مَرَّاتٍ كَثِيْرَةً بِلُطْفِكَ الْعَمِيْمِ وَاجْعَلْنِيْ فِيْهِ مُفْلِحًا يَا اَرْحَمَ الرَّاحِمِيْنَ.

O Allah, do not make this my last opportunity at this great standing place and grant us the opportunity of returning to it many, many times with Your absolute kindness and make me successful in it. O Most Kind of those who show mercy.

اَللّٰهُمَّ ارْضَ عَنِّى فَاِنْ لَّمْ تَرْضَ عَنِّى فَاعْفُ
عَنِّى فَقَدْ يَعْفُو الْمَوْلٰى وَهُوَ غَيْرُ رَاضٍ ۔

O Allah, be pleased with me and if You are
not happy with me than (at least) forgive
me for surely the Master forgives even
when He is not Happy.

اَللّٰهُمَّ لَا تَدَعْ فِى مَقَامِنَا هٰذَا ذَنْبًا اِلَّا
غَفَرْتَهٗ وَلَا عَيْبًا اِلَّا سَتَرْتَهٗ وَلَا هَمًّا اِلَّا
فَرَّجْتَهٗ وَلَا كَرْبًا اِلَّا كَشَفْتَهٗ وَلَا دَيْنًا اِلَّا
قَضَيْتَهٗ وَلَا عَدُوًّا اِلَّا كَفَيْتَهٗ وَلَا فَسَادًا اِلَّا
أَصْلَحْتَهٗ وَلَا مَرِيضًا اِلَّا عَافَيْتَهٗ وَلَا غَآئِبًا
اِلَّا رَدَدْتَهٗ وَلَا حَاجَةً مِّنْ حَوَآئِجِ الدُّنْيَا

وَالْاٰخِرَةِ لَكَ فِيْهَا رِضًا وَلَنَا فِيْهَا صَلَاحٌ اِلَّا

قَضَيْتَهَا يَاۤ اَرْحَمَ الرَّاحِمِيْنَ ۔

O Allah, do not leave for us in this place of ours any sin except that you have forgiven it, nor any weakness but You have covered it, nor a misfortune but You have removed, nor hardship but You have taken away, nor a debt which You repaid, nor an enemy but You have sufficed him, nor any corruption but You have corrected it, nor anyone ill but You have granted him relief, nor any missing person but You have returned him, nor any need from amongst the needs of this world and the Hereafter which You are pleased and there is good for us in it but You granted it O Most Merciful of those who show mercy.

اَللّٰهُمَّ لَا تَحْرِمْ مِنِّىْ لِقِلَّةِ شُكْرِىْ وَلَا تَخْذُلْنِىْ

لِقِلَّةِ صَبْرِى وَاِنْ يَّمْسَسْكَ اللهُ بِضُرٍّ فَلَا

كَاشِفَ لَهُ اِلَّا هُوَ وَاِنْ يُّرِدْكَ بِخَيْرٍ فَلَا رَآدَّ

لِفَضْلِهِ يُصِيْبُ بِهِ مَنْ يَّشَآءُ مِنْ عِبَادِهِ وَهُوَ

الْغَفُوْرُ الرَّحِيْمُ ۔

O Allah, do not deprive me (of Your
Grace) due to my lack of thankfulness and
do not disgrace me owing to my minimal
patience "And if Allah afflicteth you, none
can remove it except Him and If He
blesseth you none can reject His Grace.
He benefitteth whom He pleases amongst
His servants. He is the Forgiving, the
Merciful."

اَللّٰهُمَّ مَنْ مَّاتَ مِنَّا فَاغْفِرْلَهُمْ وَ نَوِّرْ

قُبُوْرَهُمْ وَانِسْ وَحْشَتَهُمْ وَابْعَثْهُمْ اٰمِنِيْنَ

مِنْ عِقَابِكَ مَعَ الَّذِينَ اَنْعَمْتَ عَلَيْهِمْ مِنَ النَّبِيِّينَ وَالصِّدِّيقِينَ وَالشُّهَدَآءِ وَالصَّالِحِينَ وَمَنْ مَّعِىَ هٰهُنَا فَاهْدِنَا فِيْمَنْ هَدَيْتَ وَعَافِنَا فِيْمَنْ عَافَيْتَ وَتَوَلَّنَا فِيْمَنْ تَوَلَّيْتَ وَقِنَا شَرَّ مَا قَضَيْتَ فَاِنَّكَ تَقْضِىْ وَلَا يُقْضٰى عَلَيْكَ ۔

O Allah, those who die amongst us forgive them and fill their graves with light, make pleasant their loneliness, raise them (on the Day of Judgement) safe from Your Punishment with those whom you have favoured amongst the Prophets, the Truthful, the Martyrs and the Pious.

Those who are here with me guide us like those whom You have guided, save us

with those whom You have saved,
befriend us like those whom You have
befriended and save us from the evil that
You have ordered for surely You order and
are not ordered around.

اَللّٰهُمَّ لَا تُظْهِرْ خَطِيْئَتِيْ لِأَحَدٍ مِّنَ
الْمَخْلُوْقِيْنَ وَلَا تَفْضَحْنِيْ بِهَا عَلٰى رُؤُوْسِ
الْعَالَمِيْنَ۔

O Allah, do not expose my wrong to
anyone amongst the creation and do not
disgrace me due to it in front of all.

اَللّٰهُمَّ أَنْتَ الْمَلِكُ لَا اِلٰهَ اِلَّا أَنْتَ وَأَنَا
عَبْدُكَ ظَلَمْتُ نَفْسِيْ وَاعْتَرَفْتُ بِذَنْبِيْ فَاِنَّهُ
لَا يَغْفِرُ الذُّنُوْبَ اِلَّا أَنْتَ وَاهْدِنِيْ لِأَحْسَنِ

الْاَخْلَاقِ وَلَا يَهْدِي لِاَحْسَنِهَا اِلَّا اَنْتَ وَ
اَصْرِفْ عَنِّي سَيِّئَهَا فَاِنَّهُ لَا يَصْرِفُ سَيِّئَهَا
اِلَّا اَنْتَ لَبَّيْكَ وَسَعْدَيْكَ وَالْخَيْرُ كُلُّهُ
بِيَدَيْكَ تَبَارَكْتَ وَتَعَالَيْتَ اَسْتَغْفِرُكَ وَ
اَتُوْبُ اِلَيْكَ.

O Allah, You are the Supreme Master. There is no diety (worthy of worship) except You and I am Your slave. I have wronged my soul and admit my sins. None can forgive sins except You.

Guide me to the best of manners and none can guide to the best of it except You. Turn away from me the evil for surely the evil cannot be deflected by anyone except You.

I am Present.

I am at Your service

All Good is in Your Hands.

Blessed and Most High are You.

I seek Your Pardon and I repent unto You.

اَللّٰهُمَّ اِنَّا نَسْئَلُكَ مِنْ كُلِّ خَيْرٍ مَا سَاَلَكَ

مِنْهُ نَبِيُّكَ مُحَمَّدٌ صَلَّى اللهُ عَلَيْهِ وَسَلَّمَ وَ

نَعُوْذُبِكَ مِنْ كُلِّ شَرٍّ مَا اسْتَعَاذَكَ مِنْهُ

نَبِيُّكَ صَلَّى اللهُ عَلَيْهِ وَسَلَّمَ ۔

O Allah, we seek from You all the good which Your Nabi Muhammad ﷺ sought from You and we seek Your Protection in you from all the evil that Your Prophet Muhammad ﷺ sought protection from,

اَسْتَغْفِرُ اللهَ الَّذِیْ لَا اِلٰهَ اِلَّا هُوَ الْحَیُّ الْقَیُّوْمُ وَاَتُوْبُ اِلَیْهِ۔

I seek pardon from Allah, there is no god
besides Him, the Immortal the Eternal and
I repent unto Him.

اَللّٰهُمَّ اَنْتَ رَبِّیْ لَا اِلٰهَ اِلَّا اَنْتَ خَلَقْتَنِیْ وَاَنَا
عَبْدُكَ وَاَنَا عَلٰی عَهْدِكَ وَوَعْدِكَ مَا
اسْتَطَعْتُ اَعُوْذُ بِكَ مِنْ شَرِّ مَا صَنَعْتُ اَبُوْٓءُ
لَكَ بِنِعْمَتِكَ عَلَیَّ وَاَبُوْٓءُ بِذَنْبِیْ فَاغْفِرْلِیْ
فَاِنَّهُ لَا یَغْفِرُ الذُّنُوْبَ اِلَّا اَنْتَ۔

O Allah, You are my Lord, there is no god
except You. You have created me and I am
Your slave.

I am (acting) on Your Vow and Promise to the best of my ability.

I seek protection in You from the evil I have committed.

I admit Your Favour upon me and I also admit my sin so forgive me.

Surely none can forgive sins except You.

The above dua is called Sayyidul Istighfar (The Leader of the Repentance Prayer). This is the most excellent repentance narrated to us by Rasulullah ﷺ.

To be read daily (morning and evening) throughout the year.

اَللّٰهُمَّ اغْفِرْلِيْ وَارْحَمْنِيْ وَارْزُقْنِيْ وَعَافِنِيْ ۔

O Allah, forgive me, have mercy on me, grant me sustenance and save me.

رَبَّنَا تَقَبَّلْ مِنَّا إِنَّكَ أَنْتَ السَّمِيعُ الْعَلِيْمُ۔

Our Lord! Accept (our deed/requests) from us. Surely You are the Hearer and the Knower.

اَللّٰهُمَّ صَلِّ عَلٰى مُحَمَّدٍ وَّعَلٰى اٰلِ مُحَمَّدٍ كَمَا صَلَّيْتَ عَلٰى اِبْرَاهِيْمَ وَعَلٰى اٰلِ اِبْرَاهِيْمَ اِنَّكَ حَمِيْدٌ مَّجِيْدٌ۔ اَللّٰهُمَّ بَارِكْ عَلٰى مُحَمَّدٍ وَّعَلٰى اٰلِ مُحَمَّدٍ كَمَا بَارَكْتَ عَلٰى اِبْرَاهِيْمَ وَعَلٰى اٰلِ اِبْرَاهِيْمَ اِنَّكَ حَمِيْدٌ مَّجِيْدٌ۔

O Allah, shower Your Mercy on Muhammad ﷺ and His family/followers as You showered Your Mercy on Ibrahim عليه الصلاة والسلام and His family/followers. Surely, You are the Praiseworthy and Most High.

O Allah, bless Muhammad ﷺ and His family/followers as You have blessed Ibrahim عليه الصلاة والسلام and His family/followers.

Surely You are the Praiseworthy and Most High.

سُبْحَانَ رَبِّكَ رَبِّ الْعِزَّةِ عَمَّا يَصِفُونَ ۝ وَسَلَامٌ عَلَى الْمُرْسَلِينَ ۝ وَالْحَمْدُ لِلّٰهِ رَبِّ الْعَالَمِينَ ۝

Glory be to You, the Lord of Honour, He is free from what they ascribe unto Him.

Peace be upon all the Prophets and all praise is due to Allah, the Lord of the Universe.

(25) TO MUZDALIFAH

اَللّٰهُمَّ اِلَيْكَ اَفَضْتُ وَفِيْ رَحْمَتِكَ رَغِبْتُ وَمِنْ سَخَطِكَ رَهِبْتُ وَمِنْ عَذَابِكَ اَشْفَقْتُ

فَاقْبَلْ نُسُكِى وَاَعْظِمْ اَجْرِى وَتَقَبَّلْ تَوْبَتِى
وَارْحَمْ تَضَرُّعِى وَاسْتَجِبْ دُعَائِى وَاَعْطِنِى
سُؤْلِى.

O Allah, to You I return, to Your Mercy I
turn, from Your Anger I shudder, from
Your Punishment I fear, so accept my
rites, make great my reward, accept my
repentance, have mercy on my humility,
accept my prayer and grant my request.

(26) AT MINA

اَللّٰهُمَّ اِنَّ هٰذِهٖ مِنًى وَقَدْ اٰتَيْتُكَ وَاَنَا عَبْدُكَ
وَابْنُ عَبْدِكَ اَسْئَلُكَ اَنْ تَمُنَّ عَلَىَّ بِمَا مَنَنْتَ
بِهٖ عَلٰى اَوْلِيَآئِكَ وَاَهْلِ طَاعَتِكَ وَاَنْ تَجْعَلَنِى
مِنْ عِبَادِكَ الصَّالِحِيْنَ يَا اَرْحَمَ الرَّاحِمِيْنَ.

O Allah, surely this is Mina. I have come to You, Your slave and the son of Your slave. I ask You to favour me with that which you have favoured Your friends and Your obedient ones and to make me from amongst Your pious slaves, O Most Merciful of those who show mercy.

(27) WHEN STONING

بِسْمِ اللهِ اللهُ اَكْبَرُ رَغْمًا لِلشَّيْطَانِ وَرِضًى لِلرَّحْمٰنِ۔

اَللّٰهُمَّ اجْعَلْهُ حَجًّا مَبْرُوْرًا وَّ ذَنْبًا مَّغْفُوْرًا وَّ سَعْيًا مَّشْكُوْرًا۔

In the name of Allah - Allah is the Greatest. A humiliation for shaitan and for Allah's Pleasure.

O Allah, make it an acceptable Haj and (my) sins forgiven and (my) effort a thankful (one).

(28) BEFORE SLAUGHTERING THE ANIMAL

اِنِّی وَجَّهْتُ وَجْهِیَ لِلَّذِیْ فَطَرَ السَّمٰوٰتِ وَالْاَرْضَ حَنِیْفًا وَّمَاۤ اَنَا مِنَ الْمُشْرِكِیْنَ، اِنَّ صَلٰوتِیْ وَ نُسُكِیْ وَ مَحْیَایَ وَمَمَاتِیْ لِلّٰهِ رَبِّ الْعَالَمِیْنَ، لَا شَرِیْكَ لَهٗ وَبِذٰالِكَ اُمِرْتُ وَاَنَا مِنَ الْمُسْلِمِیْنَ، اَللّٰهُمَّ تَقَبَّلْ مِنِّیْ هٰذَا النُّسُكَ وَاجْعَلْهُ قُرْبَانًا لِّوَجْهِكَ وَ عَظِّمْ اَجْرِیْ عَلَیْهَا۔

Verily, I have set my face firmly towards Him who has created the heavens and earth and I am not of those who join partners (unto Allah). Surely, my worship, my sacrifice, my living and my dying are for Allah, Lord of the Universe. He has no partner, with that I am commanded and I am among the Muslims.

O Allah, accept from me this sacrifice and make it a means of closeness unto Your Countenance and magnify (increase) my reward for it.

(29) WHEN ABOUT TO SLAUGHTER

بِسْمِ اللهِ اَللهُ اَكْبَرُ

In the name of Allah, Allah is the Greatest.

(30) CUTTING OR SHAVING THE HEAD

اَلْحَمْدُلِلّهِ عَلَى مَاهَدَانَا، اَلْحَمْدُ لِلّهِ عَلَى مَا اَنْعَمَ بِهِ عَلَيْنَا، اَللّهُمَّ هٰذِهٖ نَاصِيَتِيْ فَتَقَبَّلْ مِنِّيْ وَاغْفِرْلِيْ ذُنُوْبِيْ اَللّهُمَّ اغْفِرْلِيْ

وَلِلْمُحَلِّقِيْنَ وَالْمُقَصِّرِيْنَ يَا وَاسِعَ الْمَغْفِرَةِ۔

اٰمِيْن

All praise is due to Allah upon that which He guided us. All praise is due to Allah for that which He favoured us with.

O Allah, this is my forehead so accept it from me and forgive my sins.

O Allah, forgive me, those who shave their heads and also those who cut hair O Reservoir of Mercy.

اَلْحَمْدُ لِلّٰهِ الَّذِیْ قَضٰی عَنَّا نُسُكَنَا اَللّٰهُمَّ

زِدْنَا اِیْمَانًا وَّ یَقِیْنًا وَّ تَوْفِیْقًا وَّ عَوْنًا

وَّاغْفِرْلَنَا وَلِاٰبَآئِنَا وَ اُمَّهَاتِنَا وَالْمُسْلِمِیْنَ

اَجْمَعِیْن۔

All praise is due to Allah, who made us complete our Haj rituals.

O Allah, increase us in belief, conviction, opportunity (to do good) and support. Forgive us, our fathers, mothers and all Muslims.

اَللّٰهُمَّ اَثْبِتْ لِىْ بِكُلِّ شَعْرَةٍ حَسَنَةً وَّامْحُ عَنِّىْ بِهَا سَيِّئَةً وَّارْفَعْ لِىْ بِهَا عِنْدَكَ دَرَجَةً وَّ صَلَّى اللهُ عَلَى النَّبِىِّ الْكَرِيْمِ تَسْلِيمًا كَثِيْرَةً.

O Allah, confirm for me one good for each hair and remove for me through it one sin and raise me through them (the hair) in status in Your Presence. May Allah shower His Blessings and Salutations on the Noble Prophet.

(31) TAWAFUZ ZIYARAH
(Same duas as in Tawaf)

(32) TAWAFUL WADA‘A
(also any other duas of Tawaf)

اَللّٰهُمَّ الْبَيْتُ بَيْتُكَ وَالْعَبْدُ عَبْدُكَ وَابْنُ عَبْدِكَ وَابْنُ اَمَتِكَ حَمَلْتَنِى عَلٰى مَا سَخَّرْتَ لِى مِنْ خَلْقِكَ حَتّٰى سَيَّرْتَنِى فِى بِلَادِكَ وَ بَلَّغْتَنِى بِنِعْمَتِكَ حَتّٰى اَعَنْتَنِى عَلٰى قَضَآءِ مَنَاسِكِكَ فَاِنْ كُنْتَ رَضِيْتَ عَنِّى فَازْدَدْ عَنِّى رِضًا ۔

O Allah, the House (the Ka‘bah) is Your House and this slave is Your slave and the son of Your bondsman and bondswoman. You have conveyed me upon that which You have controlled amongst Your creation upto (the time) You brought me

into Your country. You sent me forward
with Your blessings until You assisted me
on the completion of Your rites, so if You
are pleased with me, increase Your
Pleasure for me.

اَللّٰهُمَّ فَاصْحِبْنِى الْعَافِيَةَ فِىْ بَدَنِىْ وَ الْعِصْمَةَ

فِىْ دِيْنِىْ وَآحْسِنْ مُنْقَلَبِىْ وَ ارْزُقْنِىْ طَاعَتَكَ

مَا اَبْقَيْتَنِىْ وَ اجْمَعْ لِىْ خَيْرَىِ الْاٰخِرَةِ وَ الدُّنْيَا

اِنَّكَ عَلٰى كُلِّ شَىْءٍ قَدِيْرٌ ۔

O Allah, make safety my partner in my
body and innocence (a partner in) my
religion and make pleasant my return and
make me obedient unto You. Keep me
(alive) and gather for me the good of (this)
world and the Hereafter. Surely You have
power over everything.

AFTER TAWAFUL WADA'A

اَللّٰهُمَّ ارْزُقْنِى الْعَوْدَ بَعْدَ الْعَوْدِ الْمَرَّةَ بَعْدَ
الْمَرَّةِ اِلٰى بَيْتِكَ الْحَرَامِ وَاجْعَلْنِى مِنَ
الْمَقْبُوْلِيْنَ عِنْدَكَ يَا ذَاالْجَلَالِ وَالْاِكْرَامِ ۔
اَللّٰهُمَّ لَا تَجْعَلْهُ اٰخِرَالْعَهْدِ مِنْ بَيْتِكَ
الْحَرَامِ وَاِنْ جَعَلْتَهٗ اٰخِرَالْعَهْدِ بِهٖ فَعَوِّضْنِى
عَنْهُ الْجَنَّةَ يَا اَرْحَمَ الرَّاحِمِيْنَ وَصَلَّى اللّٰهُ عَلٰى
خَيْرِ خَلْقِهٖ مُحَمَّدٍ وَّ اٰلِهٖ وَصَحْبِهٖ اَجْمَعِيْنَ ۔

O Allah! Grant me return after return, one
opportunity after another to Your Sacred
House and make me amongst the accepted
ones in Your Presence O Possessor of
Majesty and Honour. O Allah! Do not make

this the last occasion with Your Sacred Home and if You make it the last opportunity with it, so grant me in place of it Jannah. O Most Merciful of those who show mercy. May Allah shower His Blessings on His Best Creation, Muhammadﷺ, His family and all His followers.

Other Places

(33) AL-MA'ALA GRAVEYARD OF MAKKAH

اَلسَّلَامُ عَلَيْكُمْ اَهْلَ الدِّيَارِ مِنَ الْمُؤْمِنِيْنَ وَالْمُسْلِمِيْنَ وَاِنَّا اِنْ شَآءَ اللهُ بِكُمْ لَا حِقُوْنَ ۔ نَسْئَلُ اللهَ لَنَا وَلَكُمُ الْعَافِيَةَ ۔

Peace be upon resters of this place (who) are believers and Muslims. And surely, Inshallah, we will join you. We ask Allah for your and our pardon.

AT SAYYIDAH KHADIJAH'S GRAVE

سَلَامٌ عَلَيْكِ يَا اَوَّلَ اَكْمَلِ اُمَّهَاتِ الْمُؤْمِنِيْنَ اِقْتِرَانًا بِهِ وَاَكْمَلَهُنَّ وَفَاءً لَهُ وَ اَكْثَرَهُنَّ تَضْحِيَةً لِاَجْلِهِ سَلَامٌ عَلَيْكِ مِنْ كُلِّ اَبْنَاءِكِ الْمُؤْمِنِيْنَ ۔ رَضِيَ اللّٰهُ عَنْكِ وَ اٰلِ بَيْتِ رَسُوْلِ اللّٰهِ اَجْمَعِيْنَ ۔

Greeting (Salutations) upon You the First of the Perfect Mothers of the Faithful attached to the Nabi ﷺ. The Most Perfect in obedience to Him ﷺ and Most Excessive in sacrifice to His Cause. Salutations be upon You from all Your believing offspring. May Allah be pleased with You and the family of the Rasul ﷺ.

(34) ON THE WAY TO MADINAH

اَللّٰهُمَّ صَلِّ عَلٰى مُحَمَّدٍ وَّعَلٰى اٰلِ مُحَمَّدٍ كَمَا

صَلَّيْتَ عَلٰى اِبْرَاهِيْمَ وَعَلٰى اٰلِ اِبْرَاهِيْمَ

اِنَّكَ حَمِيْدٌ مَّجِيْدٌ۔ اَللّٰهُمَّ بَارِكْ عَلٰى مُحَمَّدٍ

وَّعَلٰى اٰلِ مُحَمَّدٍ كَمَا بَارَكْتَ عَلٰى اِبْرَاهِيْمَ

وَعَلٰى اٰلِ اِبْرَاهِيْمَ اِنَّكَ حَمِيْدٌ مَّجِيْدٌ۔

O Allah, shower Your Mercy on Muhammad ﷺ and His family/ followers as You showered Your Mercy on Ibrahim عليه الصلاة والسلام and His family/followers. Surely, You are Praiseworthy and Most High.

O Allah, bless Muhammad ﷺ and His family/followers as You have blessed Ibrahim عليه الصلاة والسلام and His family/followers. Surely, You are Praiseworthy and Most High.

(35) OUTSIDE MADINAH

اَللّٰهُمَّ هٰذَا حَرَمُ نَبِيِّكَ فَاجْعَلْهُ وِقَايَةً لِّيْ مِنَ النَّارِ وَاَمَانًا مِّنَ الْعَذَابِ وَسُوْءِ الْحِسَابِ۔

O Allah! This is Your Prophet's Sanctuary therefore make it a protection for me from the fire and a safety from punishment and an evil reckoning.

(36) SALAAM TO RASULULLAH ﷺ

اَلصَّلٰوةُ وَالسَّلَامُ عَلَيْكَ يَا رَسُوْلَ اللهِ

اَلصَّلٰوةُ وَالسَّلَامُ عَلَيْكَ يَا حَبِيْبَ اللهِ

اَلصَّلٰوةُ وَالسَّلَامُ عَلَيْكَ يَا خَيْرَ خَلْقِ اللهِ

اَلصَّلٰوةُ وَالسَّلَامُ عَلَيْكَ اَيُّهَا النَّبِيُّ وَرَحْمَةُ

اللهِ وَبَرَكَاتُهُ

يَارَسُوْلَ اللهِ اِنِّيْ اَشْهَدُ اَنْ لَّا اِلهَ اِلَّا اللهُ

وَحْدَهُ لَا شَرِيْكَ لَهُ

وَاَشْهَدُ اَنَّكَ عَبْدُهُ وَرَسُوْلُهُ

وَاَشْهَدُ اَنَّكَ بَلَّغْتَ الرِّسَالَةَ

وَاَدَّيْتَ الْاَمَانَةَ

وَنَصَحْتَ الْاُمَّةَ

فَجَزَاكَ اللهُ خَيْرًا

جَزَاكَ اللهُ عَنَّا اَفْضَلَ مَا جَازٰى نَبِيًّا عَنْ

اُمَّتِهٖ

Peace and blessings be upon you O
Messenger of Allah

Peace and blessings be upon you O Beloved of Allah

Peace and blessings be upon you O Best Creation of Allah.

Peace and blessings be upon you O Prophet and the Mercy of Allah and His Blessing.

O Prophet of Allah! I bear witness that there is none worthy of worship besides Allah, Who is Alone and has no partner.

And I also bear witness that You are His Slave and Messenger.

And I also bear witness that You passed the message.

You have discharged the trust (given by Allah)

You have counselled the people

May Allah reward You well.

May Allah reward You on our behalf better than which Allah rewarded any prophet on behalf of his ummah.

(37) SALAAM TO ABU BAKR رَضِىَ اللهُ تَعَالٰى عَنْهُ

اَلسَّلَامُ عَلَيْكَ يَا خَلِيْفَةَ رَسُوْلِ اللهِ

اَلسَّلَامُ عَلَيْكَ يَا صَاحِبَ رَسُوْلِ اللهِ

فِي الْغَارِ اَبَابَكْرِ الصِّدِّيْقِ، جَزَاكَ اللهُ عَنْ

اُمَّةِ مُحَمَّدٍ خَيْرًا ۔

Peace be upon you O deputy of Rasulullah

Peace be upon you O Companion of Rasulullah in the Cave Abu Bakr Siddiq رَضِىَ اللهُ تَعَالٰى عَنْهُ

May Allah reward you well on behalf of the ummah of Muhammad صَلَّى اللهُ عَلَيْهِ وَسَلَّم.

(38) SALAAM TO UMAR رَضِىَ اللهُ تَعَالَى عَنْهُ

اَلسَّلَامُ عَلَيْكَ يَا اَمِيْرَ الْمُؤْمِنِيْنَ السَّلَامُ

عَلَيْكَ يَا عِزَّ الْإِسْلَامِ وَالْمُسْلِمِيْنَ عُمَرَبْنَ

الْخَطَّابِ الْفَارُوْقَ جَزَاكَ اللهُ عَنْ اُمَّةِ مُحَمَّدٍ

خَيْرًا ۔

Peace be upon you O Leader of the faithful

Peace be upon you O Pride of Islam and the Muslims, Umar bin Khattab Al-Farooq رَضِىَ اللهُ تَعَالَى عَنْهُ

May Allah reward you well on behalf of the ummah of Muhammad ﷺ.

(39) COMBINED SALAAM TO ABU BAKR رَضِىَ اللهُ تَعَالَى عَنْهُ AND UMAR رَضِىَ اللهُ تَعَالَى عَنْهُ

اَلسَّلَامُ عَلَيْكُمَا يَا ضَجِيْعَىْ رَسُوْلِ اللهِ وَ

رَفِيقَيْهِ وَوَزِيرَيْهِ وَجَزَاكُمَاللّٰهُ أَحْسَنَ الْجَزَآءِ۔

Peace be upon you O Two Resters
(besides) Rasulullah, his Two Companions
and Ministers. May Allah reward the two
of you an excellent reward.

(40) SALAAM TO RASULULLAH ﷺ ON BEHALF OF OTHERS

اَلسَّلَامُ عَلَيْكَ يَا رَسُوْلَ اللّٰهِ مِنْ .... يَسْتَشْفِعُ بِكَ اِلٰى رَبِّكَ۔

Peace be upon you O Messenger of Allah
from ...... (name). He is requesting you to
plead to Your Lord on his behalf.

(38) SALAAM TO UMAR رَضِيَ اللهُ تَعَالَى عَنْهُ

اَلسَّلَامُ عَلَيْكَ يَا اَمِيْرَ الْمُؤْمِنِيْنَ السَّلَامُ عَلَيْكَ يَا عِزَّ الْإِسْلَامِ وَالْمُسْلِمِيْنَ عُمَرَبْنَ الْخَطَّابِ الْفَارُوْقَ جَزَاكَ اللهُ عَنْ اُمَّةِ مُحَمَّدٍ خَيْرًا ۔

Peace be upon you O Leader of the faithful

(41) DUA AT THE BLESSED GRAVE OF RASULULLAH ﷺ

(Facing the grave, recite the following, thereafter make dua to Allah for your needs. Without lifting your hands.

وَلَوْ اَنَّهُمْ اِذْ ظَّلَمُوْا اَنْفُسَهُمْ جَآءُوْكَ
فَاسْتَغْفَرُوا اللهَ وَاسْتَغْفَرَ لَهُمُ الرَّسُوْلُ
لَوَجَدُوا اللهَ تَوَّابًا رَّحِيْمًا ۝

And if they did wrong then came to you and sought forgiveness from Allah and the Prophet sought forgiveness for them, they will find Allah Most Forgiving and Merciful. *[Surah Nisa:64]*

(42) AT UHUD

اَلسَّلَامُ عَلَيْكَ يَا سَيِّدَنَا حَمْزَةَ
اَلسَّلَامُ عَلَيْكَ يَا عَمَّ رَسُوْلِ اللهِ

اَلسَّلَامُ عَلَيْكَ يَا اَسَدَ اللهِ وَاَسَدَ رَسُوْلِهٖ

اَلسَّلَامُ عَلَيْكُمْ يَاشُهَدَآءُ يَا سُعَدَآءُ يَا نُجَبَآءُ

يَانُقَبَآءُ يَا اَهَلَ الصِّدْقِ وَالْوَفَآءِ اَلسَّلَامُ

عَلَيْكُمْ يَا مُجَاهِدِيْنَ فِیْ سَبِيْلِ اللهِ

اَلسَّلَامُ عَلَيْكُمْ بِمَا صَبَرْتُمْ فَنِعْمَ عُقْبَی

الدَّارِ ـ اَلسَّلَامُ عَلَيْكُمْ يَا شُهَدَآءُ اُحُدٍ كَآفَّةً

عَامَّةً وَرَحْمَةُ اللهِ وَبَرَكَاتُهٗ ـ

Peace be upon you O our leader Hamzah,
Peace be upon you O Uncle of the Prophet
of Allah ﷺ.

Peace be upon you O Lion of Allah and
Lion of His Prophet ﷺ.

Peace be upon you O Martyrs,

O Blessed Ones, O Noble ones.

O People of Truth and Faithfulness.

Peace be upon you O Strivers in the path of Allah. Peace be upon you in return for that which you persevered. How excellent is the final home.

Peace be upon all of You, O Martyrs of Uhud and Allah's Mercy and His Blessings (be upon you).

(43) AT AL-BAQI
(Graveyard of Madinah)

اَلسَّلَامُ عَلَيْكُمْ يَا اَهَلَ الْبَقِيْعِ۔

اَلسَّلَامُ عَلَيْكُمْ يَا دَارَ قَوْمٍ مُؤْمِنِيْنَ۔ وَاِنَّا

اِنْ شَآءَ اللهُ بِكُمْ لَاحِقُوْنَ۔ نَسْأَلُ اللهَ لَنَا

وَلَكُمُ الْعَافِيَةَ۔

اَللّٰهُمَّ اغْفِرْ لِاَهْلِ الْبَقِيعِ ۔

اَلسَّلَامُ عَلَيْكُمْ وَرَحْمَةُ اللهِ وَبَرَكَاتُهُ ۔

Peace be upon you O Dwellers of Baqi.

Peace be upon you, dwelling of the Believers.

Surely Allah willing, we will join you.

We ask Allah safety for you and us.

O Allah, forgive the people of Baqi.

Peace be upon you and the blessings and mercy of Allah.

SALAAM TO THE MOTHERS OF THE FAITHFUL (BAQI)

(Ummuhatul Mu'mineen – Wives of the Nabi ﷺ)

سَلَامٌ عَلَيْكُنَّ آيَّتُهَا الْاُمَّهَاتِ الطَّاهِرَاتِ

الْكَامِلَاتِ الْمُكَمِّلَاتِ ۔

سَلَامٌ عَلَيْكُنَّ مُجْتَمِعَاتٍ مِّنْ كُلِّ اَبْنَاءِ كُنَّ

الْمُؤْمِنِيْنَ اِلٰى يَوْمِ الدِّيْنِ ۔

رَضِىَ اللهُ عَنْكُنَّ اَجْمَعِيْنَ ۔

Salutations be upon You O Pure and
Perfect Mothers. Greetings be upon all of
You from every believing follower until
the Day of Reckoning. May Allah be
pleased with all of you.

(44) SALAAM TO UTHMAN رضى الله تعالى عنه
(Grave situated in Al-Baqi)

اَلسَّلَامُ عَلَيْكَ يَا اَمِيْرَ الْمُؤْمِنِيْنَ

اَلسَّلَامُ عَلَيْكَ يَا اِمَامَ الْمُسْلِمِيْنَ

اَلسَّلَامُ عَلَيْكَ يَا عُثْمَانَ بْنَ عَفَّانَ

اَلسَّلَامُ عَلَيْكَ وَرَحْمَةُ اللهِ وَبَرَكَاتُهُ ۔

Peace be upon you O Leader of the faithful.

Peace be upon you O lmam of the Muslims.

Peace be upon you O Uthman, son of Affan.

Peace be upon you and the blessings and mercy of Allah.

(45) ON LEAVING MADINAH

اَللّٰهُمَّ لَا تَجْعَلْ هٰذَا اٰخِرَالْعَهْدِ بِنَبِيِّكَ وَ مَسْجِدِهٖ وَحَرَمِهٖ وَيَسِّرْلِيَ الْعَوْدَ اِلَيْهِ وَالْعُكُوْفَ لَدَيْهِ وَارْزُقْنِيَ الْعَفْوَ وَالْعَافِيَةَ فِى الدُّنْيَا وَالْاٰخِرَةِ وَرُدَّنَا اِلٰى اَهْلِنَا سَالِمِيْنَ غَانِمِيْنَ اٰمِنِيْنَ ۔ بِرَحْمَتِكَ يَاۤ اَرْحَمَ الرَّاحِمِيْنَ ۔

O Allah! Do not make this the last occasion with Your Prophet, His Masjid and His Sanctuary. Make easy my return to Him ﷺ and to stay in His presence ﷺ Grant me forgiveness and safety in this world and the hereafter and return us to our people safe and rewarded with Your Mercy. O Most Merciful of those who show Mercy. Amien.

OUTSIDE YOUR HOMETOWN
(The usual travel duas whilst on your way home).

لَا اِلٰهَ اِلَّا اللهُ وَحَدَهُ وَحَدَهُ لَا شَرِيكَ لَهُ لَهُ الْمُلْكُ

وَلَهُ الْحَمْدُ وَهُوَ عَلٰى كُلِّ شَىْءٍ قَدِيرٌ، اٰئِبُوْنَ

تَائِبُوْنَ عَابِدُوْنَ سَاجِدُوْنَ لِرَبِّنَا حَامِدُوْنَ،

صَدَقَ اللهُ وَعْدَهُ وَنَصَرَ عَبْدَهُ وَهَزَمَ

الْاَحْزَابَ وَحْدَهُ.

There is none worthy of worship besides Allah who is Alone and has no partner. His is the Kingdom and for Him is all Praise and He has power over everything. (We are) Returning, repenting, worshipping, prostrating and praising our Lord. Allah has fulfilled His Promise, assisted His slave and defeated the combined groups all alone.

Abdullah ibn Abbas رَضِىَ اللهُ تَعَالَى عَنْهُمَا relates from the Prophet ﷺ that Five (types) of duas are accepted :

(i)   The call of the oppressed until he is assisted.

(ii)   The prayer of the Haji until he returns.

(iii)   The Mujahid (warrior) until he completes (his Jihad).

(iv) The call of the sick one until he has recovered.

(v) The prayer of a fellow Muslim for his absent brother. *[Baihaqi]*

Anas رضى الله تعالى عنه relates that the Prophet of Allah ﷺ said, "Dua (prayer) is the essence of worship" *[Tirmizi]*

IMPORTANCE OF DUAS

① And when My servants question you about Me – behold I am near. I answer the call of him who calls unto Me. *[Quran 2:186]*

② They (Nabi Zakariya) would vie with one another in doing good deeds and would call unto us in yearning and awe: and they were always humble before us.
[Quran 21:90]

③ Who is it that responds to the distressed when he calls out to Him and who removes the evil?
[Quran 27:62]